4-29-08

D0880869

A Robbie Reader

How To Convince Your Parents You Can...

Care For A Pet Snake

Jim Whiting

Mitchell Lane
PUBLISHERS

P.O. Box 196
Hockessin, Delaware 19707
Visit us on the web: www.mitchelllane.com
Comments? email us: mitchelllane@mitchelllane.com

Printing   1   2   3   4   5   6   7   8   9

A Robbie Reader/How to Convince Your Parents You Can...

Care for a Pet Chameleon
Care for a Pet Chimpanzee
Care for a Pet Mouse
Care for a Pet Snake
Care for a Pet Tarantula

Library of Congress Cataloging-in-Publication Data

Whiting, Jim, 1943-
  Care for a pet snake / by Jim Whiting.
      p. cm. — (A Robbie reader)
  Includes bibliographical references.
  ISBN-13: 978-1-58415-604-8 (library bound)
  1. Snakes as pets—Juvenile literature. 1. Title.
  SF459.S5W48 2008
  639.3'96—dc22
                                                          2007000791

ABOUT THE AUTHOR: Jim Whiting has been a remarkably versatile and accomplished journalist, writer, editor, and photographer for more than 30 years. A voracious reader since early childhood, Mr. Whiting has written and edited more than 250 nonfiction children's books on a wide range of topics. When he was young, he captured a snake and brought it home (something you should never do), but it soon escaped. He has always wondered what happened to it. More recently, several of his friends have had pet snakes and he has enjoyed watching them. He lives in Washington State with his wife and two teenage sons.

PHOTO CREDITS: All photographs © 2008 JupiterImages Corporation.

PUBLISHER'S NOTE: The facts on which this story is based have been thoroughly researched. While every possible effort has been made to ensure accuracy, the publisher will not assume liability for damages caused by inaccuracies in the data, and makes no warranty on the accuracy of the information contained herein.

PLB

TABLE OF CONTENTS

Words in **bold** type can be
found in the glossary.

Snakes such as this rainbow boa don't consume their prey by chewing it. Instead, they dislocate their jaw to make their mouth large enough to easily swallow their meal. After eating one mouse, the boa will not need to eat again for over a week.

Chapter One

SO YOU THINK YOU WANT A PET SNAKE?

Many people are very afraid of snakes. They believe all snakes are evil, dangerous killers, but this belief is not based on facts. The truth is that most snakes are harmless to humans. In fact, many snakes help humans by eating rodents and other pests. They are very important in keeping a healthy environment.

As more and more people are discovering the truth about these animals, snakes are becoming more popular as pets. It is estimated that more than two million families now have pet snakes.

One reason for their popularity is that there are many different kinds of snakes. They vary in size, color, habits, and even the way that they behave.

Snakes don't need a lot of room. Most of the ones that would make a good first pet will need a container only about the size of a medium or large fish aquarium.

As long as their container is kept clean, snakes don't smell bad. They certainly don't bark or make other loud noises. They don't need to be taken for walks. Most snakes can go a week or two between feedings.

Most snakes are content to live by themselves. They don't need the same level of attention that dogs and cats do. But if you want, you can take a pet snake out of its container every day and play with it for a while.

Many people have **allergies** (AA-lur-jeez) to common pets such as dogs, cats, or even hamsters. Allergies are strong reactions to certain substances. These reactions include sneezing, runny nose, skin rashes, and watery eyes. They are caused by **dander** (DAN-dur) in animal fur. Dander is old skin cells that flake off. Snakes don't produce dander, so they don't cause allergies.

Like many people, you may think that snakes are slimy and cold. In reality, snake skin is quite smooth and soft. It's also likely to be warm.

A closeup view of of a boa constrictor's skin shows that it is actually made up of many tiny scales. The scales feel smooth and dry.

Learning about snakes will help you become more aware of your environment. If you keep a snake, you will come to respect it. You will understand that it has as much right to live as any other animal.

It's very important that you find out everything about your new pet before you actually get one. The best way to do this is to sit down with your parents and learn about the snake together. That can be a lot of fun.

Western blind snakes are found throughout the western United States and Mexico. Also known as thread snakes, they are almost completely blind and grow to about a foot long. They may burrow up to 50 feet into the ground in search of termite nests and anthills, their primary sources of food.

Chapter Two

ABOUT SNAKES

Scientists have identified about 3,000 different kinds of snakes. They live in almost every country in the world. Only three countries don't have snakes: Ireland, New Zealand, and Iceland.

Snakes come in many different sizes. Some may grow to a length of nearly 30 feet, though some other kinds are less than a foot long. One of the smallest known snakes is the Reuters (ROY-turz) blind snake, which lives on the island of Madagascar. It is only about five inches long.

The longest known snake is the **reticulated** python (reh-TIH-kyoo-lay-ted PY-thon). It grows up to 33 feet long and lives in Southeast Asia. The world's heaviest snake is the anaconda (ah-nuh-KON-duh). Anacondas can weigh more than 400 pounds each. Anacondas live in South America.

They usually grow to 30 feet long, though one captured specimen was 37 feet long.

Humans, other mammals, and birds produce their own body heat, but snakes do not. Some people say that snakes are "cold-blooded." That doesn't mean that their blood is actually cold. It means that snakes get the heat they need by taking on the temperature of their environment. That's why so many are found in countries that are warm. There the snakes don't have to worry about freezing.

fun FACTS

Poisonous snakes often strike in self-defense. They may not inject venom if the intruder is too large to eat. This is called a "dry bite."

In places where it gets cold during the fall and winter, snakes **hibernate** (HY-bur-nayt). They find a place to hide. Then they go to sleep for several months. When the weather gets warmer, they wake up and become active again.

Snakes control their body tempature. In the morning, they may lie on a hot rock to get warm.

As the day heats up, they'll crawl someplace shady. They may even burrow underground. In the evening, they might return to the rock where they began the day. The rock may still be warm from the sun.

Snakes are **carnivores** (CAR-nih-vorz). This means they eat other animals. Snakes can't chew, so they have to swallow their **prey** (PRAY) whole. These prey animals can range from crickets and earthworms to large animals such as pigs and deer. To do that, they **dislocate** (DIS-loh-kayt) their jaws. That allows their mouths to open wide enough.

Rattlesnakes, like other snakes, need warmth to survive. Sometimes they will lie on a rock that has been warmed by the sun.

Some snakes kill their prey by constricting it. They wrap themselves around the prey and squeeze. Soon the victim can't breathe anymore. Other snakes have a powerful poison called venom (VEH-num). The snake bites its prey and injects venom into the wound. The venom quickly kills the prey.

Smell is the most important sense that snakes use to detect their prey. Snakes do not really have noses. They use their forked tongue as a way of "smelling" what is around them.

The eyesight of snakes is usually good. Their eyes are best for detecting motion. Often a snake will move past a motionless animal that it would normally attack. Snakes can also hear, but this sense isn't very

Water moccasins, also known as cottonmouths, are poisonous. Nearly all of them live in the southeastern United States.

This garter snake has just begun the process of molting, or shedding its old skin. Soon this skin will peel all the way back and be discarded. The snake's new and slightly larger skin is already in place.

well developed. They make up for it by detecting very slight vibrations in the earth around them.

The way that snakes grow is interesting. Their bodies are covered with a skin that consists of heavy scales. These scales help to protect snakes from injury. However, the scales won't expand very much, which prevents the snake from growing.

How does the snake solve this problem? A new set of larger scales grows beneath the existing ones. A snake has to get rid of its skin to free this new set. It begins the process by rubbing the corners of its mouth against a rough surface such as a rock or tree trunk. That breaks the old skin, which begins to come loose. Then the snake wriggles out of its old skin. Young snakes will do this several times a year.

Tri-colored hognose snakes are popular pets that are native to Bolivia in South America. They are available in the United States through snake breeders. They rarely reach two feet in length, so they don't need much room. They are also known as false coral snakes because their coloration resembles that of the very poisonous coral snake. However, the tri-colored hognose snake is harmless.

Chapter Three

CHOOSING A PET SNAKE

Many people think that the best way of getting a pet snake is to capture one. For example, you might find a garter snake in your yard and want to keep it. There are several reasons why you shouldn't.

In many places, it is illegal to capture a wild snake. This is especially true of snakes that are **endangered** (en-DAYN-jerd).

Wild snakes are more likely to have some sort of disease and to be more aggressive. After a life in the wild, it can be difficult to adapt to living in a container.

Capturing a snake can be dangerous unless you know for certain that the snake is not venomous. For example, some types of milk and king snakes—some of the most common pet snakes—look a lot like venomous coral snakes.

Therefore, you should always buy your snake from a pet store or a person who specializes in breeding snakes. Many cities and states have **herpetological** (hur-puh-tuh-LAH-jih-kul) societies. *Herpetological* comes from a Greek word that means "crawling." A herpetological society is a group of people who have pet snakes. Most of these groups are listed on the Internet. Members enjoy sharing their knowledge. They can help you find a person who breeds snakes.

Breeders have snakes that do well in captivity. These include garter snakes, ribbon snakes, corn snakes, king snakes, and a number of other kinds. Breeders are likely to have lots of information about caring for each kind of snake.

There are several things to look for when you select a snake. It should look alert, with eyes that are bright and shiny. Its tongue should frequently flick in and out. There shouldn't be any wounds on its skin. Never purchase a shedding snake. If you think you might want a snake that's shedding when you first see it, it's better to wait and come back after the process is complete.

Some breeders may try to sell you a sick snake. You see the snake and feel sorry for it. You believe that you can make it better.

This is not a good reason to adopt a snake. You probably won't be able to make it better, and it could become very expensive if you have to take it to a **veterinarian** (veh-truh-NAYR-ee-un).

The best way to bring your snake home is in a pillowcase or cloth bag. The cloth allows air to circulate so that the snake can breathe. Make sure that the top is tied securely. It would be very distracting for your parents if the snake got out of its bag while they were driving!

Corn snakes, like many snakes, lay eggs. A newly hatched albino corn snake shows the bright red eyes of its breed. Corn snakes occur in several colors and are known to be mild-mannered, which makes them easy to handle.

Chapter Four 4

TAKING CARE OF YOUR NEW PET

The most important part in taking care of your new pet snake is the container in which it will live. Snakes usually don't move around very much, so they don't need a lot of room. The container only needs to be about the same length as the snake will be when it is full grown. You'll want a container that has a glass front so that you can watch your pet. It also has to have plenty of **ventilation** (ven-tih-LAY-shun) so that air can flow smoothly.

You can make your own container, but most people buy them in a store. Either way, you have to make sure that the container is completely sealed, especially at the corners. Your snake needs only a tiny opening to escape. There are several things that you will have to put inside the container.

Your snake has to keep warm, so you'll need to buy some type of heater. Being able to control

A red-tailed boa at home in its cage. This pet's owner has provided moss, a branch, and other surfaces on which it can climb. The lamp in the back will keep the snake warm.

its body temperature is just as important to pet snakes as it is to snakes in the wild. For that reason, one side of the container should be slightly cooler than the other side. It's a good idea to have a thermometer at each end.

A snake also needs light. The best kind of lighting is fluorescent (fluh-REH-sent). It is the most similar to sunlight, which provides healthful vitamins for snakes.

fun FACTS

If your jaws were as elastic as a snake's, you could eat something the size of a basketball. Even a big hamburger would go down with one bite.

Another thing is a hide. A hide is a small place where your snake feels completely safe, especially when it is about to shed its skin. Many pet stores sell inexpensive hides. You can also make one yourself. A cardboard box with a small hole in it makes a good hide.

Water is absolutely essential. Your pet has to have a source of drinking water. Snakes also like to soak themselves, so you need a bowl that is big enough to hold the snake's entire body as it takes its "bath."

You may also want some decorations, such as a tree branch lying at the bottom of the cage. You can also add another branch for your snake to crawl up, but be sure that this crawling branch is securely fastened.

It's important to make the container easy to clean. You can line it with newsprint or paper

In 2006, a pet python swallowed an electric blanket that was being used to keep the snake warm. The cords in the blanket are shown in the X-ray (top right). Veterinarians had to perform a two-hour operation to remove the blanket.

towels. Once a week, remove the paper and replace it. You don't want to use sand or bark, which can contain tiny insects that could harm your pet.

Feeding your pet can be difficult, especially at first. Some people don't like to put live animals into the snake's cage, knowing that they will soon be eaten. There is another reason for not feeding your snake live prey. It can fight back and inflict a painful wound on your snake.

The best solution is pre-killed prey. These are animals that are already dead. They can be kept in your freezer. They need to be defrosted and slightly warmed before putting them in the snake's container.

At first, your pet may not want to eat dead prey. If not, you can use a pair of tongs to wiggle the dead animal back and forth in front of your snake. You can also dip the prey in chicken broth. *Never* hold your snake's food in your fingers, as this can lead to a bite.

Like other animals, snakes can catch harmful diseases. Keep a close eye on your pet for the first sign of anything wrong. Vomiting, diarrhea (dy-uh-REE-uh), and weight loss are some signs of poor health. The best way of preventing disease is to regularly clean the container.

It is a good idea to keep a record of important events in your pet's life. These events include when the snake is fed, when its container is cleaned, and when it sheds its skin. This record will be very useful for the veterinarian who takes care of your snake.

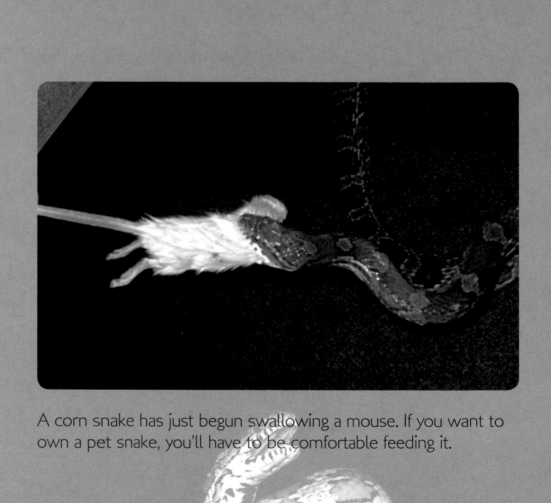

A corn snake has just begun swallowing a mouse. If you want to own a pet snake, you'll have to be comfortable feeding it.

Chapter Five

SUMMING UP

Now that you know more about snakes, you can decide if you still want one as a pet. One of the biggest objections to having snakes is their diet. Some people just don't like to handle the little animals that snakes eat, whether they're alive or already dead. You have to make up your own mind about this.

Just like any other pet, having a snake is a long-term commitment. Snakes that are well treated can easily live for ten years or even longer. You cannot release an unwanted snake into the wild. It probably won't survive very long. The only good way of getting rid of a snake you don't want anymore is finding someone to adopt it. That could take a lot of time and energy.

This cage awaits its new occupant, a boa constrictor. Newsprint on the floor of the cage makes it easy to clean. The upturned crates at each end make excellent hides, or places where the snake can conceal itself.

Snakes won't show affection like other pets. They won't wag their tails or purr if you play with them.

But there are many good things about having snakes as pets. One is that they are completely dependent on you to take care of them.
It can be very satisfying as the weeks and months and years go by that your snake is still healthy.

Another good reason for having a snake is telling your friends and classmates the truth about snakes. This is very important, because many people still are afraid of harmless snakes. This may especially be true of your parents. As they learn about snakes, perhaps one day they will even be willing to handle your pet.

You can also tell them that you will take good care of your snake. Most parents realize that caring for a pet is good for their children. It helps them to develop a sense of responsibility.

fun FACTS

The world's fastest snake is the black mamba. It is a poisonous snake that lives in southern Africa. It can go as fast as 12 miles an hour.

And you can tell them about all the advantages a pet snake has. It doesn't need much space. It is easy to care for. It will teach you a great deal. It's fun and exciting to watch the behavior of a creature that most people hardly ever see.

Deciding whether to have a snake for a pet is really a two-step process. First you have to convince yourself that you really want one. Then you have to convince your parents. Good luck!

Books

Craats, Rennay. *Caring for Your Snake*. New York: Weigl Publishers, 2004.

Oberon, Jake. *Snakes as a New Pet*. Neptune City, New Jersey: T.F.H. Publications, 1990.

Pringle, Laurence. *Snakes! Strange and Wonderful*. Honesdale, Pennsylvania: Boyds Mills Press, 2004.

Vrbova, Zuza. *Snakes: Junior Pet Care*. Neptune City, New Jersey: T.F.H. Publications, 1990.

Works Consulted

Allen, E. Ross. *How to Keep Snakes in Captivity*. St. Petersburg, Florida: Great Outdoors Publishing Company, 1971.

Flank, Lenny Jr. *Snakes: Their Care and Keeping*. New York: Howell Book House, 1998.

Geus, Armin. *The Proper Care of Snakes*. Translated by Christa Ahrens. Neptune City, New Jersey: T.F.H. Publications, 1992.

Griehl, Klaus. Snakes: *Giant Snakes and Non-Venomous Snakes in the Terrarium*. Translated by Rita and Robert Kimber. Woodbury, New York: Barron's Educational Series, 1984.

Smith, Hobart M. Snakes as Pets. Neptune City, New Jersey: T.F.H. Publications, 1980.

Care of Snakes http://www.ahc.umn.edu/rar/MNAALAS/Snakes.html#VetExam
Feeding Pet Snakes—Prekilled or Live Prey http://exoticpets.about.com/od/snakes/f/snakesliveprey.htm
How Snakes Behave http://www.petplace.com/reptiles/how-snakes-behave/page1.aspx
Lovgren, Steven. "Huge, Freed Pet Pythons Invade Florida Everglades." National Geographic News, June 3, 2004.
http://news.nationalgeographic.com/news/2004/06/0603_040603_invasivespe.html

Web Addresses

Are You Ready for a Pet Snake? http://www.talktothevet.com/ARTICLES/REPTILES/index.html
Choosing a Pet Snake and Snake Environment http://www.animalcareassociates.com/snakepet.html
Garter Snakes as Pets http://www.aboutsnakes.com/garter_snakes/gartersnakesaspets.html

allergies (AA-lur-jeez)—strong reactions to certain substances such as pet dander; reactions may include sneezing, runny nose, skin rashes, or watery eyes.

carnivores (CAR-nih-vorz)—animals that eat other animals.

dander (DAN-dur)—old skin cells that flake off animals and remain in their fur or get into the air as dust.

dislocate (DIS-loh-kayt)—to move a bone away from its normal position in relation to another bone.

endangered (en-DAYN-jerd)—threatened with danger or extinction.

herpetological (hur-puh-tuh-LAH-jih-kul)—having to do with the study of snakes.

hibernate (HY-bur-nayt)—to go into a deep sleep during which the body processes slow way down.

prey (PRAY)—animals eaten by other animals.

reticulated (reh-TIH-kyoo-lay-ted)—joined together in a netlike pattern.

ventilation (ven-tih-LAY-shun)—a way of providing fresh air.

veterinarian (veh-truh-NAYR-ee-un)—a doctor who specializes in treating animals.